BALLINTRILLICK
IN THE LIGHT OF BEN WHISKIN

Letry '07

To Ronald & Martha.
Love,
Bernadette.

BALLINTRILLICK
IN THE LIGHT OF BEN WHISKIN

TOM MORGAN

Tom Morgan   Christmas 2006.

LAGAN PRESS
BELFAST
2006

Acknowledgements
Force Ten, Windows, Belfast News Letter, The Sligo Champion and
Fortnight.
Some of these poems were also part of a joint poetry-painting-music
exhibition with the artist Catherine McWilliams and the composer
Frank Lyons entitled 'Ballintrillick in the Light of Ben Whiskin' as part
of the Visonic Arts Festival at the Ormeau Baths Gallery, Belfast.
Again, thanks to Dermot Healy—a hard task-master—for his help in
getting this MS together. Always patiently encouraging, his imagination
helped to improve technical matters but threw light on areas of the
mind and heart I wasn't aware of.
I am also indebted—in more ways than I can possibly list here—to
Francis Crean for his interest, knowledge and sense of humour.

Published by
Lagan Press
1A Bryson Street
Belfast BT5 4ES
e-mail: lagan-press@e-books.org.uk
web: lagan-press.org.uk

ARTS
COUNCIL
of Northern Ireland

ISBN: 1 904652 36 0
Author: Morgan, Tom
Title: Ballintrillick in the Light of Ben Whiskin
2006

Design: December
Printed by J.H. Haynes, Sparkford

for
Bernie, Darragh and Niamh-Áine

There are two kinds of simplicity, the
Simplicity of going away and the simplicity of
Return. In the final simplicity we don't care
Whether we appear foolish or not. We talk of things
That earlier would embarrass. We are satisfied with
Being ourselves, however small.

—Patrick Kavanagh

Contents

Ballintrillick
for Mary Kate, John Patrick and the Magowan family

At my garden's edge a fuchsia bush stirs
in a holy amber light flung from far Atlantic.
The place is eerie, still; now pagan, then Christian,
whatever one might will; green edging purple, gold
under a crescent moon as it slopes to Muckrim;
down the mearn wall to stir the bogwood
and the curlew in Derrylehon.

Coolagraphy

No need to beat your head against a wall,
no need for the brain to fry in its own juice.
Lie on your back and look at the sorrel,
or sit up and feel air move free and loose
over dog-daisies below the thorn hedge;
or feel sap rise and fall over the ledge into
The Duff where meeting the waters in June
all is shimmering under the bluest sky;
the back of the dried moorland sweet with hay,
the mind drifting to its home in Coolagraphy.

Carrig

i.m. Spencer Bonney

I

Beneath a balcony
the pianist's fingers
barely touch the keys.

We look down and sigh;
the hall is full; this
is where we come to learn
to grow bald gracefully.

II

Behind the altar
a wide window
frames mountains
trees and sky.

How can the priest
preach each Sunday
with such sunlight
in his eyes?

Tibawn

I

Most of all I love the whitethorn,
its back bent to the bare headland
like mine each black dying morn,
holding on by the skin of my teeth.

II

To the west a golden sun,
to the east storm clouds;
to the north beyond the Border,
the sky a deadly mood swing.

Bealtaine I mBallintrillick
for Ray Duncan

For three days mist has capped the mountain.
From Gleniff to Glenade the old road skirts
the hill of graves where fleeting sunlight
fires whins tumbling downhill
past the ring fort and still sheep—
a painter's brush daubing blankets of green—
where, under the half-rusted tin of an old house,
primroses tucked under ferns, stumps of trees.

All is still inside. A monitor reflects
the brass-and-iron bed, a bowl for washing,
the smell of newly-ironed sheets.
Above my head, a spider moves across
open rafters and a starling wrecks silence
under the tiled brown roof.

For five days I have discarded tablets.
Tonight I hope for sleep after my turbulent mind
deals with a deadly past; the graveyard
at Conwal stealing the end of day,
white water seeping from ground under my feet.

Carrawakee

Somehow we arrived.
A tin roof letting starlings in,
ragged doors at front and rear—
right-of-ways for snails and wind—
a mound of heaped ashes
patted like shiny ice;
the shell of an old Morris,
a perfect chicken coop;
dockins, nettles under rhododendrons.

Everything untouched, unfinished:
two sheds with bulging walls;
one for turf, one for dogs and hay;
children bleaching feet through dew;
neighbours at harvest
laughing the hind leg off you.

Now we are porched, flushed and wired.
The timekeeper has left for dirt
and a police car shines lights
through bedroom windows.
The door is on the latch
for no one to enter.

Little import to the life
of the nation, tribunals, or money
changing hands under polished tables.
I might be alone at the crossroads
staring at the butt of a ditch,
or, eyes ablaze, baying at the moon.

Oughtagorey

Light brightens as
bells ring at St. Brigid's;
a neighbour bends his knee,
lifts a hand from head to heart.
Children are gone
leaving a heavy mind,
a rusty swing on a rotted tree
where our dog barks
at distant thunder.
To hear the clock chime
over the open hearth is bitter-sweet.
Stone walls, ring-forts, Earl-Rua's Pass
are filled with presences.
The spire on the church is like
an exclamation on pagan things.
Twin perfume stills another panic attack.
This place would exhaust
the last star in the galaxy.
I rise, go to the door, keep out
rain with my tattered mac.

Tus na hOige

A boy of ten
sits in a run-down caravan,
cradles a gun on his knee
and peers out the broken window.
The carnival is in town
and rain has stopped.
He watches drops run
down a railing fence,
meet in the middle
in a globe of rainbows,
until, too heavy, it falls
down the veins of dockins.
Dodgems have started
under the noisy merry-go-round.
When he peers again,
a robin sits on a rusty engine.
His being trembles!
He opens the gun,
pushes a dart inside,
aims through the broken glass
and pulls the trigger.
The bird flies up leaving
thunder in his ears.

Ganuach

A car sits at a house;
a cat stands with a frog in its mouth.
Behind hills the unanswerable
drone of the sea. The new baby
lives in a grape seed
and a mother is brittle with fears.
Grief I learnt will grow old before
the new moon is a half-eaten melon
and flowers disappear in clouds of poison.
I try to repeat myself in the dawn
but slipped on a heap of ashes,
dug medicine bottles in stony corners.
We live on borrowed things where
breeze's architecture nurtures its element.
Dance, sing; for life comes in pincer movements.
Look hard at the magpie,
see its powerful flight
over grass and veins in skin
to score the land's anguished bidding.

Coileach

I watch this morning
a ten year girl explain
the art of Bridget's Cross.

At her side my daughter and son
eagerly watching, gently hum.

Beyond this square of peace,
snowdrops light the ground,

nod cowled heads against
brown bones of a fox's head
wind has just blown down.

Mullannahu

I

My house is in a hollow,
lobster-shaped, sucking down.
I keep my window closed
to breathe at night.

II

Was it to dream well
that a man next to me,
pulled a ladder up after him
and slammed the wooden trap door?

Edencullentragh

When she married the servant boy
they fell into disgrace.
Her madness, her eccentricity
were brushed aside and her daughter
hearing the news, drowned in the tide.

One morning she made stirabout
and left it on the frosty ground to cool.

A calf skittered as a neighbour passed
but Madam only laughed at wonder in his face.

She scooped the cow-pat and flung it on the grass
laughing like a man, smacking hands, making deals;
'What the human eye can't see,' she yelled,
'the human heart can't feel!'

Glaisintawee

All seemed lost.
From east to west,
from mountains to sea,
a leaden sky
pressed hard on lobes
with its humid grip.
A car roared past
and dust settled.
All seemed dead
but for water over stones
under the grey bridge
where a fish shook lilies.

Suddenly a scattering.
With a flash of coloured plumage
a kingfisher flew from whins
like a tyrant scene-breaker,
its dagger-like bill
diving a dark pool,
into hysteria;
rose again on dead air
like sun coming out
lifting the heart;
a misericord for the spirit.

Clumballoon

I

> When he touched his cap
> at the priest near church,
> he realised at last he was too long
> carrying the landlord's pisspot.

II

> It is too much
> to feel this high
> all year long
> like a manic depressive.

Annacoona

Dear Anna crying; the night the stranger stood in your midst
you took your husband's hand and left the gathering, crossed
marshy land to the mountain, felt the ground slipping
under you as you made your way to a gap in Skib, where,
lying on dewy sprit under a frosty sky, you felt the baby moving,
your man beside you whispering comfort as you pushed
    and gasped
until your bloodied daughter lay on petticoats flung awry.
And when she cried, you heard the sound of hooves under as
your husband crept to the edge of the cliff, saw soldiers dismount,
slaughter neighbours from lowlands who felt safe in the booley.
You tried to warn of fear as your daughter's cries were almost
choked to death as yells for mercy stabbed the hills when soldiers
left all dead including the stranger from Manorhamilton.
Years later with Una strong you went to the waterfall, lay on
the Monrock to rest but fell asleep that night and slept
    too long; woke
cursing rushes withered and dead, useless for roofing
    or making light.

Anach

When the well-dressed lady
on the steps before the stream
ate her leg of chicken
with certain delicate charm,
and looking up at me
remarked on the new Ulster man
who wears the latest silk shirts
under perfect British diphthongs:

I spun my own cocoon, and,
like the old Chinese,
hid my skills at weaving
for three thousand years
in gossamer threads on mulberry leaves.

'Nil aon tintean mar do thintean fein'

The river of trees is still.
Ben Wiskin tips the sky
like a sharp Chinese painting.
On the dash of the gable wall
Virginia creeper
looks like Picasso
killing a farmer.
Bernie's voice echoes the kitchen;
a place she made
to love and grow in;
soothe the mind,
banish desolate times.

Lubog Beag

Under firs and arc lamps
shapes move downhill
where ewes' bellies shiver.
It is nearly Easter
and lambs come
with teeth in their eyes.
Moon turns an old car
into a stream of silver;
in an empty barn a dog barks,
like myself, surplus to requirement.
Stunted blackthorn don't sing
and last year's butterfly
is still in the jug on the window.
Yellow and purple pansies
bear a hoar frost;
dandelions' ragged feet
trample dying primroses.
A child with a river's face
cries in a new house.
We are on an edge.
Shadows struggle uphill,
where it is hard to sleep,
harder to stay awake.
Like the lamb in the dewy grass
it is time to grow a new beard.

Poll Cormac

'He owned a pub, garage
and funeral parlour.

When he went into politics,
people said given half a chance,
he'd even bury your dandruff.

"Street angel; house devil."

I make sure when he comes
I give him no tea, for,
like the auld cats
you'd only be bringing
them about the house.'

Tobar Hearneach

The priest banged the pulpit;
'Cats and dogs are at it
and people follow after
in lounge bar and parlour!'

Jimmy eyed his sister
on the other side of the aisle,
her left eye twitching
at the allusion in his style.

Mass ended slowly,
the crowd walked away;
Mary pedalled quickly
like every other Sunday.

The dunghill needed heaping,
the place was all awry,
turmoil in her freckled breast
mocked an ice-blue sky.

She piled potatoes in the pot
and brushed the dusty floor;
Father Murphy grinned
as his car passed her door.

Wind tossed hedges,
petals fell from the rose;
loneliness stole quietly
down the darkened road.

Mary lit a candle
and slowly went to bed;
she fingered beads blindly,
built a crannog in her head.

Croiz

I

Over blind ewes,
swallows like burnt grey paper
freed upon the air.

II

To find a language to be proud of
beyond pointing fingers and the garrulous;
dream song thickens in Croiz.

Bainne Gloc

There's a makeshift canvas tent
on the edge of a vanishing lake.
To the north are mountains,
to the rear, bog and sea.

I stop to watch the water's level
when a traveller lifts his canvas door,
draws his feet through dew,
picks berries from the brambly hedge;

sun flashing gold
off a brass-and-iron bed
on a woman upright on a mattress,
nets and paper on her head.

Garawa

Where were ya last night?
Jimmy's
Doin what?
Talkin.
About wimen?
Naw.
Should have flutes cut off ya
and lave ya with holes
for sloshing outa.

Baile Bui

It is hard on hips,
it is cold on bones;

it is hard
to make ground soft
sleeping on stones,
without the threat of water
hosed in the early morning.

Pee against the wall,
hold on to the stars;
room for you, me
and the shrews.

Cashel

Miles from the heart of power
where eyes are glazed with money,
and love is another investment—
whins explode gold;
whitethorn is delicate china;
electric swallows skim bog water
near my stony sterling days.
An otter free-falls in a drain,
its shiny body arching uphill
where a pup barks in an echoey barn.
The curlew cries with its holly crown,
and the sea's roar never sleeps.
There is a dead fox
a dead badger,
and a priest sings over his collar.
Someone cries in the countryside
as the first leaves fall
on silent fiddle strings.
Do these things wrestle
to make sense of the world
with their silent moving arms;
or does the croaking frog feel
the urge of rain dance?
I don't need to urge them on;
for the wind, moon and sun,
second by second, day by day,
with no investment of mine
will let drowned eyes sleep
in pieces of piercing mockery.

Clough

Snow clouds over Gleniff
as one year slips into another.
At the spirit-grocer's I am wished luck
where light fades and dies.
This is where I come to be alone,
far from cities, deadly arguments
in the poisoned chalice of The North.
Someone calls and I look up
at razor-edge Ben Whiskin,
and, staring hard, I let go,
feeling dark imploding inward
like steps in Winter Snow.

Tawnach
for Darragh & Mary

From rocks under Ben Whiskin
a hoarse-voiced raven flies;
blue-black body
falling this way and that.
My neighbour looks away,
blesses himself at an ill omen
near wood avens, tufted foliage,
panicles of yellowed saxifrage.
Close by, a mist drifts over
Dairmuid and Grannia's cave
where a girl at the end of her time
hopes the moon will bring delivery.
My mind cowers before
the strength of local wisdom.
In fields above Keelogues
blood is soothed by spleenworth,
herb bonnet, bending ferns
at the side of one-eyed ewes:
land of the blind fleshing
the core of the raven's view.

Polladunsie

I

Outside our garage door
the moon moves through
a frozen cobweb and a
dog digs for its bone.

If I say dog, moon or bone,
my eyes will disappear
and my heart turn to stone.

II

The light on the primroses less
than the light on whins.

Between them, the bridge of
the dead, grey and beckoning.

Gortnahowla

On harvest Monday I backed away from the rick
winding a shaped wire through a worn spool,
the sugan fed by the knowing hands of my neighbour,
tripped and fell into Gortnahowla clachan,
its orchard long decayed, its wood spoilt and torn
for fences and fires in far away places.
Sitting upright, I eyed remains of the village.
If you walked the field, trod tractor and hoof marks,
or climbed the largest rock you would see the plan
for ten homes where nettles and weeds grew.
Gortnahowla upper and lower touched
at the glen where the Mass Rock stood.

Gurnamaile

Take, for instance, thon one
and her son just moved in.
First there were the two of them,
then a third, the son's girlfriend.
They cut the hedge like blind men,
moved to the bog and pared the bank.
Thon's a great one! After ten minutes
she's down on her arse, smoking fags,
drinking beer, muttering words like clouds
and sea while her son wastes match
after match on freshly-cut turf.

And what happened next? The son moved out
and the mother with the girlfriend
were kissing on the lawn under bells
of the church ringing the Angelus.
Should be put under ground
and a flag pulled over!
She brought bad luck here
with nothing but rain since she laughed
at her neighbours down on their knees
doing the Nine Fridays.

And what happened next? The girlfriend
moves out and her father moves in.
A painter be God. Couldn't paint his arse!
dirty shameless old whore of a one
and the state she has thon house in;
it's transported she should be.
Thinks she's a big shot; a big shite she is.
And luk at the painter; mad to get rich
and him reared on rye stirabout!

Gairedearg

In the vale of jealousy
blinding light caught eagles' rock,
sky a host of pastels in eerie Shancrock.

Air near sea
when a light moved inland
like a Whistler 'Nocturne',
mist took hold again
over cows ghoulish
in the dimmest lantern.

Terrible shock
in the narrow sward
where a sheep stood still
with a crow on its head.

Grotesque pain;
the beak fell with metal precision
bullets puncturing glass;
or the peasant girl
with hamstrings cut;
capillaries burst
at the world's black entrance ...

Crocaduine

Below the dark sky
in the sheep-bleat of evening,
ash trees move like Chinese fans.

On the road's ascent
into the green haven,
red lights of Gulban's Mountain.

Cupenagh

Something I missed down the road last night.
All day it nagged cleaning French drains,
piling dressed stones near plastic pipes.
Walking that stunted place, clawing rain
swept the bog as hedges called me in.
That feeling persists like eyes painting whins,
or tossed canawaun watching distortion
in the iron bog-water. The land runs uphill,
up the right-of-way I've avoided for a year.
It is time to dig blue daub for strong foundations,
see berries fall from rowan approved by storm;
below, a red door reflects the sunlight.

Gainetronan

The abacus is put away.
Under a festive eiderdown
my daughter's curls
spill on her cheeks,
cover the face of the circus clown.
She breathes to the tune of Jack and Jill
chasing each other from hill to hill.
Her fingers entwine hair
and a white cotton scarf
comforts neck and breast.
Above her head
the brass bed rises
through daisy-chains and ribbons
where an eastern idol
with outstretched wings
and jewelled eyes
guards from the mantelpiece
and keeps safe the night
with clear expert eyes.

Caille na Mallacht

Swallows skim willow,
stir grass, settle for seconds.
Above their wings
gulls have flown inland,
their wheeling shrieks
cutting oak and sycamore.
Is this a pet day?

In the past, signs
were clearly seen,
and my dead farmer friend
could breathe deeply,
scan the landscape, feel wind
for signs of coming weather.
Now, we could have four
seasons in one short day.

So I work on, pick thorns
from fingers, watch the endless sky,
the place sated with sound,
a thud of thunder, maybe,
or soldiers firing in Finner Camp,
making ready for Bosnia, Africa;
sights scanning strange horizons,
looking for signs of coming weather.

Lanahowna

It is hard to move forward
when the same thing happens twice.
Yesterday I lifted an English Dictionary
from a shelf beside the cooker.
Its absence made an Irish one fall.
Today it happened again.
Both fell to the floor but
the larger one opened
like a crashing door!
Inside the cover, my name in Irish.
I do not know which to turn to.

Lugnacocanestill

It was the hollow of the flaxen well, we found out.
Now wind glows sheen on laurels,
chafes sap on the swaying bluebells.

Glenade

Under the one roof they wouldn't speak,
under the one roof they wouldn't laugh.
A brother and sister in each end of the house
coming rarely together at each side of the hearth;
she in the remnants of her rocking chair,
he on the hob opposite casting insults
or spitting violently into the open turf fire.
And when she died a neighbour laid her out
while he bent and danced but never spoke or cried,
his form flitting with dying embers tossed
by western winds through icy skies.

Gurnahaugh

Sun on top of the strath,
wind in the little town.
Swamps at edge of the base,
laughter in Black Honor's place.
Signs in the wood of deaf men,
summoned to work in the commons.
Sloes at the ring of the black glen,
fun in the island of rabbits.
Blessings at the Bishop's house,
rain at the foot of Patrick's fort.
Stones at the quarter of sandbanks,
hares on the island of oysters.
Feet on the hill of murders,
choughs on top of red mountain.

Deora De

The fuchsia hedge is brown and dead.
Fields are white with hoar frost
and skies have gone to bed.

It is impossible to think flowers
or tears from God in summer sunlight.
Sap has gone underground.
How speak of petals in that caricature?

Best to break brittle stems,
light fire against risen wind,
warm hands to cool the throbbing head.

Garin Or

for Bernie

I

Every dimension right. The angle of the ladder,
the stone in the arch above the fireplace,
the half-door sanded and polished
under open rafters to give extra light;
each flagstone marked and squared;
a perfect place to measure time in.

II

The moon of the Autumn stubble
the bank of the yew,
the patch of the crock,
the fisherman's coy.
Everything its right place
except myself.

Drinaghan

Moving to clear brambles from a ditch
we saw it for the first time.
A golden patch near sally and ash,
the light on bark where it grew
shimmered leaves eerily,
buds above our heads a wild indigo.

The second time, a branch tore back,
embers sparked by the wind
near midges and starling;
on the dash of the gable wall,
on the green of fascia boards,
my family watching the first star fall.

Tooneenvalley

Between the loaded fuchsia and the broken fir,
moon falls where the road meets hedges.
Fields carry the mountain, brace Atlantic
and time is laid to rest in flooded meadows.
There is no time for cowards and shuffling badger
yearns for wheels of cars in silent badgers' corner.
Below the clasai snow is heaped on snow and
my love lies there with charcoal in her mouth.
Let water turn to mist and teach me to persist
like the mad blind poet with pots on his bag
and hands for seeing in happy wrinkled eyes.
Or my blind pet seal under the table, lifting head,
sniffing air and going under before storm;
his comic flesh moving from the lighted lantern.

Pankatober

Uplifted
by a Paul Henry sky
drifting my spirit
towards a nature God,
my stride grows.
With the bent holly
and a child with sheep's hair
winning gravel races,
I was bone-tired
with barrenness
under wild and ragged things
till the not-seeing habit
fled scutch grass,
weeds and rushes killing fields
where a heron stood still
at an ever-changing lake;
my face bumping into itself
by the new day-by-day;
uplifted by the sky.

Curraghmore

There is hay on his jumper from feeding cattle;
a hairy old crombie flaps in the wind.
His walk is slow and his talk is steady pointing
at whitethorn, rowan and sally.

He thumbs backwards and eyes North.
A place beyond his knowledge, he's a veteran
of foxes and sheep, the wind's direction
or colour of scree on the edge of the mountain.

'How are things up there?' he asks politely,
but tired to reply, I avoid its complexity,
ask about people, the mart and harvest,
who's alive or dead, mad or happy.

When his feet change from turf in the bog
he soon finds his place in the spirit-grocer's;
an empty crate with his back to the fridge
with views of the door the street and bridge.

When I ask about weather eyes me as a stranger;
his face stares the floor as he ponders his answer.
'If the new moon's on its back, it's a sign of rain;'
but how could a downpour be caught in a saucer?'

Seafur an tsiuil

This morning I walked the road
from Ned's Cross to Tawley.
Canawaun whispered
where the bog was cut out.
It felt like walking on air,
stones slipping under me.
Under a bridge the Duff flowed slowly
after a night of heavy rain.
Browns impinged on greens, blues
and swallows plunged hollows
where air was seething.
Mornings in the light of Ballintrillick;
invincible Summer was in me
and the heart travelled everywhere.

Short miles as the crow flew blood was up.
Black-suited marching men
wanted the King's highway
like they could eat it;
knuckles flailing air
sending shivers down spines.

I looked at mist painting the mountain
as my indulgence grew. If I was in power
what would I do? Let walking men
go anywhere; clap and sing to make secure;
link arms to deflate lines of deceit
for the spirit dies in these towns.

And the binding conditions?
Laughter every ten paces,
see the colours in rainbows,

love the smell of honeysuckle, roses;
feel summer sunlight banning strained faces;
wind billowing banners, birds singing
to ban the late Walpurgis-night.
I still hope for the impossible.

An Strainseir Coimhthioch

Our crafty friend is back.
From fields below Tibawn
she sings down the road
without camber or signs,
past the holy well,
her terrain the perfect stranger
silent and easily impressed.
I listen now and again
to the depth of song in her.

To the north sun sets behind
the Blue Stacks like a cardboard cut-out,
to the east a digger rumbles drains.
She sings as if in salutation
to the land's rough outline.
Welcome back; what would time be
if she wasn't urging us
and the stranger towards Summer.

Muckrim

When no quarter is given
and flowers grow grey,
my dog looks at me askance
as if behind her eyes
she knew a secret meaning.
Then cat leaps stairs,
hides in the loft.

I rise out of darkness
and move to the road.
Doc says, 'Look at infinity.'
I fix eyes on a line of sea
where islands float the horizon.
My feet stay stuck in melting tar;
another wave binds my heart
with terrible terror.

The minister honks driving past,
affable and waving.
His way could be mine,
mine his; could I live
with Moses, Abraham, Jacob?
I look at the palms of my hands;
the life-line strangely broken.

Bernie laughs in the kitchen;
she has ways to deal with most things.
I cannot see myself or her,
till I go to my seat,
and, whistling quietly, watch notes
mix with gnats in floating sunbeams.

Ceise Feilim
for Niamh-Áine & Barry

When wind from the hills threw leaves at the car
and the holly bent with its thorns from the stars;

when wind from the roads strained zinc on the roof
and fuchsia bent with its tears to its roots;

when wind from the sea tossed hay on the land
and the street at our door went mad at its hand;

when wind from Tibawn stuck clothes to my knees
and eyebrows narrowed and bark left the trees;

when wind at the gate rubbed my eyes to a glaze
and firefly and wasp and birds left with speed;

then wind blew the mist, scattered the haze,
brought rain for the weeds at the Ford of Finn's Place.

Cliag

Protestant bells ring out
over heads of Catholic youth
turning a once-green lawn
into a place for kicking.
Minister arrives smiling.

I am not one of yours
or ours but barely mine.
This changed world;
bluebells and paths of cherry blossom;
colours mixed with raucous sounds.

The listed-burnt buildings
near railings of your church
could be mine each Sunday
but for fate. Your prayers
to wish another well move
into air, drift with bells over
still waters of a lake.

The roads we take to mountains or sea
sleep quietly this Spring Sunday.
We are all survivors here
till a man in black beckons
up the mosaic floor above arms
of competent helpers
leading us to rest;

the way ahead simple,
the labels gone to
nurture the good earth, maybe.
Ring out Protestant bells.

Shancrock

I

Under the Hunter's moon,
purples and blues
ring King's Mountain.

Far below,
a mink trails two shadows
over the crossroads.

II

When cars' lights
lit the fuchsia hedge,
the road was bleeding.

Brochee

My son has my dream. After lotto numbers
are flashed on TV and a voice says:
'One and a half million,' he conducts
through the sash window—

'If I won that,' he says laughing,
'I'd hire the Berlin Phil
to play all day in Jack's Field'—
reeds between notes,
ragwort sticking to rosin and string;

players sinking into muck below their medium
where the conductor slugs poteen,
brings Sean Nos alive again
under sloes and briars at the badgers' den.

Ben Whiskin

Praying for ease beside the Atlantic,
my pine door moves with wind from the chimney.
Through pink curtains Sligo Town in the South
glows mountains behind Ben Whiskin.
My mind deceives, sees the Plough tire
of stars in their flashing freefall.
Dead father's figure stoops at my bed while
my son's restless tossing troubles joists.
Between the burning liver and the need for peace,
facts of copulation tease me to my knees.
Images come and go while whisked breath-like
vinegar troubles my face on the crumpled pillow.
Outside the window, blue stones on the road
come and go, shadow my fear and bitter love.

Leclassor

'To Live is not to resign oneself.'—Albert Camus

When the priest and teacher
tell the people beauties
of the afterlife,
I know, at last, why
drains are blocked,
wells are killed with sewage,
dogs gnaw bin-liners,
and flesh creeps to make hearts stop.

When Greeks opened Pandora's Box,
the last and greatest of human ills was Hope.
Contrary to the human mind,
hope equals resignation.

Clogher

The man in the mental
rifts and farts
and plucks the blankets.

His father
at the bedside
sighs and smiles.

'Better that, son,
than the priest's wheels
crunching the driveway
in the early hours.'

Lugnamallachee

After four weeks of drought,
a June downpour floods streets.
Orange poppies hang heads
too heavy for slender stems;
the singing thrush
on the cherry blossom
is silent again.
Birds swoop on the feeding dish,
peck and hop where the air is pure.
for the first time in weeks
my mind is clear.

La Fheile Eoin

In bed under a velux-framed sky,
eyes smarten from bonfires,
tyrannies, revolts and mayhem.
Light dims as a north wind
scuds clouds from Atlantic.
Images implode in the star-dripping night
as I pray for acceptance of 'what is'
in a different 'homeland'
where a neighbour bends a knee,
prays under a chiming clock.

Gulban's horses flee the mountain,
their hooves banished by 'Bulben'.
Outside; a rusted chain on the rotted tree—
my children's homemade hurdles—
worlds of barbed wire in me.
Days of exile, from what, from whom;
stealing places, time.
What started with beauty
and one all-consuming light
are thousands of fleeting shadows
coming and going above my head
in this longest of long nights.

Achu
for Padraic Fiacc

Ash, birch
hazel and sycamore;
bluebells, violets
dandelion.

Between our house
and the next.

The last I love.
Bane of watering cans;
ruination of lawns;
weed of the spring sun
reminds me of me.

Rain falls on frost.
Along the verge
the first primrose.

We are never satisfied.

Coil-Dubh
after Brahms
for Alan & Maddy Tongue

After the concert when notes shook the belfry and strings
like shivers ran down the spine, crows settled on oaks,
rain and wind ushered the heart back to the mountain.
How cold and bare the house; grey stones like a cave.
Outside, the mind dipped to a hollow in the flaxen well,
bog and trees barely visible on the hill's horizon.
I looked down, saw your light on the far side of the bay
come on, then off, at fifteen-second intervals. On my side
the clock was dead in the forest where darkness killed
the brooding sky and stone walls creased and crossed
    the brow.
Your light flashed again and a curlew dived over canawaun,
its sharp cry piercing river, gorse and whins.
This mood, it seems, has endured a lifetime like feet
in a dim ward or blade marks on yellow skin,
where thought, a response to memory, missed the light.
But this was your plan. Your light on like Morse
and my reply with the cars in the late evening.
Time for an end to guilt, prayer, pain; tablets
    without my name.
Above me the firmament like a perfect Allegro comodo.

Drumgawns

Light fades and dies. Under the mountain
wind scatters hedgerows and the path
to Keelogues is crow-black.

My heart stops. It is midday in winter
and with every darkness sap slips back
like the tossed dolmen in Clough,
frosty ground shrivels and cracks.

I have travelled miles
through the rubbish dump of the North,
passed the frame of a house
where light flickers in a monk's cave.

I could say the words peace, prayer;
pass cold centuries and freezing nights;
hear silence between words as ego fades,
falls and fades with the winter light.

Ahagoria

The girl beside me laughs, twists
and talks to her friend about clothes
and her daughter's back teeth.

The bus lurches uphill
towards her house and mine.

I hope she finds molars, I hope too.
On my chest under the wet coat,
I feel the pain of criss-crossed lead.

Crocaduine
for Jack the Sailor long gone

'My race a ripe grape for drunken feet.'—Franz Fanon

We have gone to strange places
aching from injustice:
hyena-men, jew-men, cafir-men;
Paddy, Mick, Gringo.

In Mexico we
marched to the tune
'Green grows the lilacs
and sweet falls the dew';

our marching cadence
taken up by clapping hands
under hopeful mouths calling:
Gringo, Gringo, Gringo!

Mullanfad

I do not see myself
carried the long street
of a town or village,
past grocer and baker,
the jaundiced face of a publican,
under flags and bunting
of any denomination.
After the furnance has eaten
plain wood and handles,
I would be put in an urn
and my ashes scattered
on a dead day
over my hardest making;
the septic tank, its strong smell
under concrete lids
to keep bacteria in,
cloying Summer air
as a handful of poets—
no masks supplied—
read poem after poem
under sycamore and ash,
not looking for rhythm or rhyme,
for that will be my will:
the big sea-captain first,
maps and territories next,
and 'look at the stars' third.
I was confined in the urn
but now I am mobile,
waiting for wind to blow me
past this wasteful energy
up mountain paths and fields
craving the sky.